Balm for the Soul

Jessica Solchenberger

BookLeaf
Publishing

Presentation by *BookLeaf Publishing*

Web: www.bookleafpub.com

E-mail: info@bookleafpub.com

ISBN: 9789357748322

First edition 2023

*To my Mom and Dad. They constantly
inspire me to grow.*

ACKNOWLEDGEMENT

I am thankful to my parents, brother, sister in law, nephew and friends. Without your support, I don't know where I'd be today.

PREFACE

These poems are every bit of me. They came about in a period of growth from chaos to calm.

With Each Drop of Rain

With each drop of rain.
I find words anew.
a feeling of clarity
or perhaps cleansing.
an, out with the old.
in with the new
type of feeling.
where the future
is open. and new.
It's all a little scary.
and yet.
with each drop of rain.
I find more to me
than I ever knew.
possible.

One Month Ago

One month ago.
my life changed.
More
than expected.
More
than planned.
And yet, I'm still here.
thriving.
learning to smile again.
laughing
more.
finding my way back
to me.
and a newer version
of a life
well lived.

Within

3

I find peace.
most often.
where
it's least expected.
and. most needed.
-within-

I hope

4

I hope.
with all my might.
you
find your light
again.

Some Days

Some days.
we may need reminders.
of the good.
Because.
sometimes. we get lost
in the dredge.
and my word.
there's so much negativity.
But. no doubt about it.
every. single. day.
there is good.

This Life

6

With each new day.
I am finding peace
and a gratitude
that I never knew possible.
This life
is everything.

I Want

7

I want
more than anything.
to be a Light.
and erase the darkness
in this world.
because. My God.
there is so much
darkness.
So. for today.
and for always.
I will do what I can
to be that light.
and bring you
out
of the darkness.

Everything Will Be Okay

8

I am so in love
with the light.
especially. the light
before
a storm.
it brings me hope
that everything
will
be
okay.

Lighter Than Air

9

Today, I feel
lighter than air
as I move. quickly,
or rather, quicker.
running through the wet streets.
the chill of the air
all around me.
the sun shining
through
the gray clouds.
taking the time
to breathe.
in.
and.
out.
so grateful.
for this moment.

Find Joy

May we all find
a little bit of
Joy
in the little bits of
light
in our days.
and. may we let it
Lift
our
souls.

I Took a Moment Today

I took a moment today.
in the chaos.
my thoughts were churning
on everything happening.
But- instead of focusing
on what went wrong today.
I found positives.
and my word. it's so important
to find these. and so different
from the last few months.
I took a moment today
and found some pride
in everything accomplished.
It was a good day.

Keep Blooming

May all our blessings
continue
blooming.
Always.

I Find Peace

I find peace.
more now
than I thought possible.
I smile. more.
I still process things.
but with more clarity
and acceptance.
I am learning that
I
am
in
a
much
better
place.
in the here and now.

she started with kindness

she was infinitely attracted
to the light others held.
wanting to share. a bit.
of her own light.
she started with kindness.

Light

15

today.
Light
is a serenade
to the deepest part
of my soul.

Everything I Need

There is something about
a bit of movement.
quick
or
slow.
in the sunlight.
that feeds the soul.
and today,
it is everything
I need.

At Peace

17

I began the day
with high hopes.
a whisper of positive vibes.
and tonight,
I end the day
on a high note.
a lovely ending, truly.
I am at peace.

Just Be

18

Take it all in.
the beauty
of a day well done.
and
just
be.

I Have Got This

19

I find myself grateful.
more than ever-
for the changes
that have come
in the last few months.
I never really knew chaos,
until my head and heart
were at war.
and now, truly.
they are at peace.
and I can keep moving
forward.
whether it be running or walking,
my new mantra is,
and will (probably) forever be,
I have got this.

All We Wish For

May our hearts
soar.
with glee.
May our minds
be filled
with contentment.
and all our days
Be
all we wish for.

My Intention

Every
single
day.
my intention is
to give a little magic
to the hearts
needing it the most.
including
my own.